This book is to be returned on or before
the last date stamped below.

LIBREX

LOUDOUN ACADEMY
EAST AYRSHIRE COUNCIL

941·1

SCOTLAND
1700–1900

RICHARD DARGIE

Explore Scottish History is packed with historical evidence  to help you discover how Scotland's people lived in the past. It also includes links to the Heinemann Explore website and CD-ROM ⊙.

Heinemann
LIBRARY

www.heinemann.co.uk/library
Visit our website to find out more information about Heinemann Library books.

To order:
☎ Phone 44 (0) 1865 888066
🖹 Send a fax to 44 (0) 1865 314091
💻 Visit the Heinemann Library Bookshop at www.heinemann.co.uk/library to browse our catalogue and order online.

First published in Great Britain by Heinemann Library, Halley Court, Jordan Hill, Oxford OX2 8EJ, a division of Reed Educational and Professional Publishing Ltd. Heinemann is a registered trademark of Reed Educational & Professional Publishing Ltd.

OXFORD MELBOURNE AUCKLAND JOHANNESBURG BLANTYRE
GABORONE IBADAN PORTSMOUTH (NH) USA CHICAGO

Designed by Celia Floyd
Originated by Dot Gradations
Printed by Wing King Tong in Hong Kong

06 05 04 03 02
10 9 8 7 6 5 4 3 2 1
ISBN 0 431 14526 1 (hardback)

06 05 04 03 02
10 9 8 7 6 5 4 3 2 1
ISBN 0 431 14527 X (paperback)

British Library Cataloguing in Publication Data

Dargie, Richard
Scotland1700–1900. – (Explore Scottish History)
1. Scotland – History – 18th century – Juvenile literature
2. Scotland – History – 19th century – Juvenile literature
I. Title
941.1'07

Acknowledgements

The Publishers would like to thank the following for permission to reproduce photographs:

Bridgeman Art Library p5, Hulton Getty pp14, 19, 23, 24, 26, 28, Mary Evans Picture Library pp15, 16, 17, 25, 27, 29, National Museums of Scotland pp18, Scotland in Focus pp6, 7, 8, 9, 10, 13, 20 (P Davies) 21 (M Moar), 22, SCRAN pp11 (National Library of Scotland), 12 (East Dunbartonshire Libraries).

Cover photograph reproduced with permission of Mary Evans Picture Library.

Our thanks to Ian Hall of the University of St Andrews for his comments during the writing of this book.

Every effort has been made to contact copyright holders of any material reproduced in this book. Any omissions will be rectified in subsequent printings if notice is given to the Publisher.

Any words appearing in the text in bold, **like this**, are explained in the glossary.

Contents

On the edge of change: Scotland in 1700

In 1700 Scotland was at peace. Most Scots lived in the countryside and worked as farmers. Gaelic was the main language of the country people. The largest town in Scotland, Edinburgh, had around 30,000 inhabitants.

After 1700 Scotland changed very quickly. Some of the old towns, especially Glasgow, grew rapidly. New factory towns grew up, thanks to changes in industries such as textiles and coal-mining. Many people left the Highlands for new lives in the **Central Belt** or overseas. The countryside also looked different as farming was changed by new methods. So many things were changing in Scotland that people at the time felt that they were living in an 'Age of **Revolutions**'.

Union with the Auld Enemy

For centuries the Scots looked on England as the 'Auld Enemy'. After the **Union of the Crowns** in 1603, the two countries shared the same **monarch** but were still separate in every other way. However, in 1707 the Scottish and English Parliaments voted to accept a Treaty of Union between the two countries. There was to be the same currency and taxes in both countries. The flags of St Andrew and St George were combined into a new Union Flag.

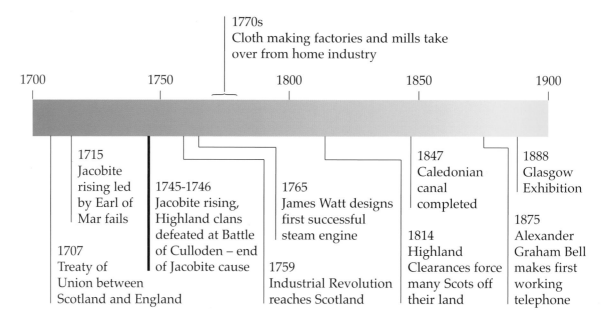

1770s
Cloth making factories and mills take over from home industry

| 1700 | 1750 | 1800 | 1850 | 1900 |

1715
Jacobite rising led by Earl of Mar fails

1707
Treaty of Union between Scotland and England

1745-1746
Jacobite rising, Highland clans defeated at Battle of Culloden – end of Jacobite cause

1765
James Watt designs first successful steam engine

1759
Industrial Revolution reaches Scotland

1847
Caledonian canal completed

1814
Highland Clearances force many Scots off their land

1888
Glasgow Exhibition

1875
Alexander Graham Bell makes first working telephone

The English wanted union to make sure that Scotland chose a **Protestant** monarch. Queen Anne was childless and old. The English wanted the Protestant George of Hanover to be king when Anne died. They worried that the Scots would instead choose the **exiled** Prince James Stuart who was a **Catholic**. This might lead to war between the two kingdoms. Some Scots wanted the union so that they could trade in England's **colonies**.

The Union with England was very unpopular. Copies of the Treaty were burned in public and there were riots against the higher taxes that Scots now had to pay. However, the nobles in the Scottish Parliament ignored these protests. Many had taken bribes and other gifts from the English government. Others hoped for well-paid jobs in London. Some genuinely believed that Union with England would be good for Scotland.

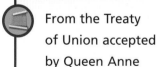
From the Treaty of Union accepted by Queen Anne in 1707

A new United Kingdom with one Union Flag
UK to have only Protestant monarchs
One Parliament in London with the Scots Parliament abolished
One system of currency, weights and measures and taxes in both countries, with the Scots pound abolished
Scotland to have only 45 MPs at Westminster
Scots allowed to trade in English ports and colonies
Scots allowed to keep their own laws and national Kirk

Exploring further

The Heinemann Explore CD-ROM will give you information about Scotland and the world from 1700 to 1900. From the Contents screen you can click on the blue words to find out about Scotland and the wider world.

The Jacobites

In 1688 King James VII had to flee into **exile** in France because he was a **Catholic** and wanted to rule without the help of Parliament. He was replaced by the Dutch **Protestant** – William of Orange. In 1715 the throne of Great Britain passed to the German Protestant House of Hanover. However, many people in Scotland stayed loyal to James and the Stuart royal family.

James Francis Stuart

As Jacobus is the Latin for James, Stuart supporters were known as Jacobites. Most of the Jacobites lived in the Highlands and the north east of Scotland.

King James VII died in 1701 and his son James Francis Stuart claimed that he was now the rightful King of Scotland. There were many plots and several armed risings to put James on the throne. His best chance came in 1715. The Rising was led by the Earl of Mar. Within weeks, over 12,000 well-armed Jacobites had 'come out' for King James.

There was great support for King James throughout the north of Scotland. However, Mar knew that his Highland army had to link up with the Jacobites in the Borders and in northern England. Only a small government army of 4000 men lay in his way at Sheriffmuir, a few miles north of Stirling.

The Jacobite and government troops clashed there on 13 November 1715. The battle was drawn but the Jacobites retreated northwards to Perth to find reinforcements and supplies. This gave the government time to send more troops to Scotland. The Jacobites' best chance of winning had gone. By the time James arrived from France in December, the Rising of 1715 had failed.

The Stuarts tried again four years later. Spanish troops were sent to Wester Ross to meet up with Jacobite **clansmen** there. However most of the Spanish ships were scattered by a storm. The few soldiers who managed to land in Scotland had to surrender to government troops after a short battle in Glenshiel.

After these Risings, the government sent General Wade to quieten the Highlands. He built forts across the Highlands and linked them with straight, fast roads. Government troops could now reach the Highland trouble-spots very quickly.

 General Wade's Bridge over the Tay at Aberfeldy in Perthshire was completed in 1735 and cost over £4000 – a huge sum at the time.

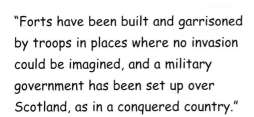 "Forts have been built and garrisoned by troops in places where no invasion could be imagined, and a military government has been set up over Scotland, as in a conquered country."

From a letter written by James Stuart in 1743

 Exploring further – Queen Anne

Read about Anne, the last Stuart monarch, on the CD-ROM. Follow this path:

Biographies > Anne.

The adventure of the Bonnie Prince

Off a rocky isle in the Outer Hebrides, a French **galleon** lay at anchor. A small group of men rowed ashore at Eriskay. One of these was the Jacobite Prince Charles Edward Stuart or 'Bonnie Prince Charlie'. The Highland chieftains who met Charles urged him to go home. Charles is said to have replied "I am come home". The Rising of 1745 had begun.

By 1745 the German princes of Hanover had ruled Britain for 30 years. Yet many Scots still secretly supported the Stuart cause. The Prince's **standard** was raised at Glenfinnan in August. Although the risks were great, several thousand **clansmen** marched with Charles Stuart to Edinburgh. Only eight weeks after landing, he had captured the capital of Scotland and defeated the government army at the Battle of Prestonpans.

In November the Prince led his men towards London. The tough Highlanders made a very rapid advance into the heart of England. By 4 December, they were at Derby, around a hundred miles north of London. The Hanoverian Court was in a panic and George II prepared to flee from the city down the Thames on a barge.

However there were few new recruits for the Prince in England. His Highland men wanted to go home to spend winter on their farms. Reluctantly, the Prince led his men northwards to Scotland. The Stuarts had lost another chance to win back their thrones.

 The Glenfinnan Monument marks the spot where Prince Charles raised the Jacobite standard on 19 August 1745. The monument was erected in 1815.

The battle lasted for little more than an hour. The Highlanders were badly **mauled** by the government guns. Charles left the battlefield in tears, knowing that his best men were dead. The wounded and the prisoners were slaughtered, where they lay, on the orders of 'Butcher Cumberland'.

THE BATTLE OF CULLODEN WAS FOUGHT ON THIS MOOR 16TH APRIL 1746.

THE GRAVES OF THE GALLANT HIGHLANDERS, WHO FOUGHT FOR SCOTLAND & PRINCE CHARLIE, ARE MARKED BY THE NAMES OF THEIR CLANS.

In Scotland, new recruits and soldiers from France doubled the Prince's army and it was still strong enough to defeat a government force at Falkirk in January 1746. However, the Government in London had time to organize a fresh army of over 10,000 experienced men with **artillery** under William Cumberland.

The last battle to be fought in Britain took place on Culloden Moor on 16 April 1746. The Jacobite troops were exhausted after a hard march the night before. The battlefield was a flat moor where the government army could use its cannon to full effect on the charging Highlanders. It was the wrong battle in the wrong place. The Jacobite cause died with those Highland soldiers.

 A Jacobite officer explains why they lost at Culloden in 1746

"The men showed eagerness to come to action but they were overpowered by a larger force and the field of battle was ill chosen, which gave Cumberland an advantage with his cannon and his horsemen."

Exploring further – Digging deeper

The Digging Deeper section of the CD-ROM takes a detailed look at the life of Bonnie Prince Charlie: Digging Deeper > Bonnie Prince Charlie

Click on the different topic headings to find out more.

Auld Reekie: Old Town and New Town

Gardyloo! 'Watch the water', shouted the people of Edinburgh as they emptied chamber pots out of their windows into the streets below. Families of ten or twelve crushed into tiny rooms that had once housed one or two. These were the sights and sounds of Old Town Edinburgh.

After the battle at Culloden in 1746, Scotland was at peace. There was more trade and the towns and cities grew quickly. The old medieval burghs were soon cramped and overpopulated. They were also dirty and unhealthy. The worst **slums** were in the high **tenement** 'lands' of Old Town Edinburgh. These medieval buildings ran down from the Castle hill to Holyrood Palace. The thick stench of people, animals and the smoke from the chimneys gave the city its nickname of Auld Reekie.

From a description of Old Town Edinburgh written in 1771

"The people throw out their impurities from their windows at a certain hour of the night. Despite the care taken by the city cleaners to remove this nuisance every morning by break of day, much of it still remains...."

Now that Scotland was at peace, there was no need to live close to the Castle for protection. In the 1760s the city council began to plan a 'new town' to the north of the medieval city. A young architect called James Craig won the competition to design a modern, spacious city.

The streets in New Town Edinburgh were straight and well lit, unlike the crooked **wynds** in the Old Town. The houses were built in the fashionable **neo-classical** style with Roman and Greek decoration.

After the 1760s, the wealthier people in all of Scotland's cities began to move to new houses away from the old districts where the poor lived. In Glasgow and Aberdeen, the rich moved to new fashionable terraces in the West End where the prevailing wind would not carry the odours of the poor and the factories left behind in the East End.

Changes on the Land

After 1730, Scottish farmers began to try out new farming ideas from Holland and England. The old **rigs** were closed off into square fields. The new fields were drained, cleared of stones and fertilized. Trees and bushes were planted around the fields to shelter young crops and animals from the biting Scottish wind. These new fields produced far better harvests.

By 1800 farming in Scotland was a very successful business. Many Scottish landowners and farmers built large, stone farmhouses and had money to spend on luxuries. However not everyone had a new, modern farm. Many of the old **fermtoun** folk lost their land and their homes in these changes. They had to leave the countryside and go off to the cities in search of work.

Crops like barley and oats were grown on these long strips of arable soil called rigs. They were raised up to keep the crops safe from wandering cattle.

Exploring further – Georgian towns

Edinburgh was not the only town to be expanded during the Georgian period. Follow this path to find out more about Georgian homes: Digging Deeper > Georgian Britain 1714 to 1837 > Houses and homes.

Scotland on the move

Before 1750 it was difficult to travel in Scotland. The roads were often just tracks which turned to mud in the rain and snow. It was especially difficult to move heavy goods. Many travellers preferred to sail around Scotland's dangerous coasts rather than get bogged down in the mud.

After 1750 farmers needed better roads to send their produce to market in the growing towns. Factory-owners needed to move heavy **raw materials** and finished goods. So businessmen got together to set up Turnpike Trusts. These were companies that built hard, well-drained roads and then charged people to use them. Over three hundred turnpike roads were built in Scotland between 1750 and 1850. They were straight, fast and didn't get washed away in the winter. It was now much easier, and cheaper, to travel across the country.

 Tolls charged on a turnpike road in 1804

Sheep, pigs, goats and lambs	6 pennies per dozen
Cattle, horses and oxen	9 pennies per dozen
Horseman	3 pennies
Coach drawn by 1 or 2 horses	2 shillings
Coach drawn by 3, 4 or more horses	4 shillings

Canals

Some very heavy goods such as coal and iron **ore** were still too bulky to move by road. Instead they were carried on the new canals. The great Iron Works at Carron near Falkirk used canals to get supplies of cheap coal from Glasgow and to ship out iron products such as guns and stoves.

 After 1850, boats such as these were used to carry coal from Monklands to Glasgow and iron products from Carron to the port of Bo'ness.

Railway fever!

The first 'railways' in Scotland were used to help horses pull heavy coal wagons. The Kilmarnock to Troon railway that opened in 1812 was one of the first in the world to be powered by the new steam engines.

By 1850, Scotland had over a thousand miles of passenger railway track. Railway lines connected every part of the country and Scots could now make journeys in hours that used to take days or even weeks. Railways were built by '**navvies**', many of them from the Highlands and Ireland. The railways created jobs for drivers, guards and signalmen, and also for those who mined the coal needed to power the trains.

 Hundreds of navvies were employed for months in building this huge railway viaduct at Glenfinnan in the Highlands.

Fast trains meant that fresh milk and other foods from country farms were carried quickly into the city. New readers across the country bought national newspapers like the *Edinburgh Scotsman*. Letters only took a day to travel from the Borders to the Orkneys. Trains also made it easier for people to travel away on holiday to new resorts such as Pitlochry and Nairn.

Exploring further – Victorian railways

The Digging Deeper section of the CD-ROM allows you to find out more about the topics that interest you: Digging Deeper > Victorian Railways gives details about the effect of this invention on daily life in Britain. Click on the topic headings to find out more.

New ways of working

In 1700 most Scots made their own linen cloth by hand. After 1770 new machines were invented that changed the way cloth was made. These machines spun more thread and wove more cloth than people ever could by hand. However, the machines were too expensive for ordinary people to buy. Instead businessmen built enormous factories or mills to house the machines. People no longer worked at home with their families but had to go and work in the mill.

 In 1700 families worked together in the home spinning their cloth. This changed when the machines came.

Discipline in the factories was strict. Workers were fined if they made mistakes and spoiled the cloth. To keep their jobs, they had to work up to fourteen hours each day. Despite this, there was no shortage of people desperate for a job in mill towns such as Paisley and Dundee.

Ports such as Arbroath, Montrose and Aberdeen imported cheap **flax** from Russia and Poland turning it into fine table linens. Mills in the Glasgow area made cotton cloth, using **raw materials** brought from America and the West Indies. By 1810, over ten million pounds of cotton were landed on Clydeside docks every year.

A traveller describes the cotton mill workers of Glasgow in 1817

"Although the city grows in prosperity, I think there are more long white faces in the Trongate than before. These are the weavers and other workers in the cotton trade. From living in a crowded town and not breathing healthy country air between their tasks, they look unwell and unhappy. Many of the young men, in the prime of life, are already ill from lung disease."

The child workers of New Lanark

Many mill-owners used children as young as five or six to look after their machines. Children were cheap to hire and easy to find. Many poor parents also needed the wages that even young children could earn. Children were also small enough to get into the machinery and clean out the dust and dirt that collected there. Sometimes they fell asleep and got tangled in the machinery. Horrible injuries, such as crushed fingers, were common.

One cotton mill was different. This was the New Lanark cotton mill owned by David Dale. This vast cotton mill was one of the largest in Europe when it was extended in 1793. Working conditions at New Lanark were better than in most factories of the time. Dale built decent houses for his workers, charging them a reasonable rent.

Dale's work was carried on by his son-in-law, Robert Owen. In 1803 Owen tried to persuade Parliament in London to pass a law reducing the hours worked by mill children. His efforts led to the first Factory Act in 1833. This made it illegal to employ children younger than nine in factories.

Robert Owen explains why he set up a school

"This school has been set up at New Lanark so that the mothers of families will be less anxious about their children and be able to earn more to support them, while the children will be prevented from acquiring bad habits and will learn the best habits instead."

Exploring further – Evidence of industry

Paintings and photographs can tell us about the changes in the way people worked. The CD-ROM includes many pictures of people at work. Follow this path: Pictures > Discoveries, Inventions and Ideas
Click on the pictures to make them bigger and find out what they show.

A new age of iron

By 1750 the population of Scotland and England was booming. More people meant there was a greater demand for all kinds of things made of iron. Iron was needed by the new factories, the new canals and on the new farms.

In 1759, three businessmen built the world's largest factory on the banks of the River Carron near Falkirk. Carron Iron Works was an amazing sight. At its busiest, it was more than a mile long and employed hundreds of skilled men. Heavy materials and finished goods were shipped by canal to the company port at Bo'ness.

In 1801 the geologist David Mushet stumbled across some strange rocks near Monklands in Lanarkshire. He had discovered Blackband Ironstone, an **ore** that was already mixed with coal and could be used to make high quality metal. Within a few years, completely new 'iron towns' such as Airdrie and Motherwell had sprung up. Their furnaces burned and smoked all day and night. Some called the area 'The Land of Fire'.

These were exciting years, when Scots led the way with new technology. It was a Scot, James Watt, who perfected the steam engine which transformed the world. The first successful passenger steamship was Henry Bell's *The Comet*, which ran down the Clyde to Glasgow in 1812.

Many new ideas and new inventions streamed out of the workshops of central Scotland. In 1890 the railway bridge over the Firth of Forth was opened. Its massive spans made it the largest iron structure in the world. Proud Scots rightly thought of their country as the 'Workshop of the World'.

From a speech given by the Provost of Glasgow in 1872

"Is there another city in the world that makes as many products as great Glasgow? Railways, engines, whole ships, iron bars, scientific instruments of every kind, from large to small, this mighty workshop on the Clyde sends out every day a thousand products which are witness to the hard work and intelligence of our citizens."

Power from the pit

In 1730 coal was still easily found on the ground in many parts of central Scotland. As more coal was used by Scotland's factories, miners had to dig ever deeper to find rich seams of coal. By 1850 most Scottish mines were over three hundred metres deep.

The youngest children worked as trappers. They sat all day in the dark of the mine, opening and closing gallery doors and shutters.

Scotland's deep mines were dangerous places and mining accidents were common. Several hundred miners died in Scotland every year. Hundreds more were seriously injured. After 1800 more coal than ever was needed, so the pits were slowly modernized. New machinery was used to ventilate the shafts and pump out water. After 1842 Parliament passed laws protecting the workers and banning the use of women and children in the mines.

A writer who visited a mine in 1869

"The miner is in constant danger. The winding gear may give way. He may be suffocated by foul air or scorched to death by the explosion of methane gas. In 1865 seventy seven lives were lost. The average weekly wage of miners in Scotland was three shillings [15p]"

Exploring further – Victorian factories

You can find out more about life in Victorian factories in the Digging Deeper section of the CD-ROM. Follow this path:

Digging Deeper > Victorian factories.

Kirk and school

In 1700 the **Kirk** and religion played a big part in peoples' lives. The minister was well respected, especially in country parishes. It was his job to make sure that the people in his parish behaved and led 'godly' lives. He was also in charge of helping the sick and the poor.

A group of men called elders helped the minister. They sat on the Kirk Session. Their job was to watch out for local people who behaved badly. Sinners who were **blasphemers** or immoral or drunken had to sit on the 'stool of **repentance**' as the minister read out their sins from the pulpit.

 Stools of repentance, like this one, would have been in churches all across Scotland. Sinners would sit on them while the minister read out what they had done wrong to the rest of the congregation.

After 1800 the Kirk began to lose its power over the Scottish people. Partly, this was because people were moving away from small country villages to live in the bigger towns. It was harder for the church to control people in the cities. Many poorer people worked in factories on the **Sabbath**, which went against the Kirk's teachings. However, the Kirk still had a lot of influence over schools in Scotland. Most teachers or 'dominies' were chosen by the minister and the Kirk Session.

 A writer describes the importance of the Sabbath, 1754

"Not long ago, a minister was in trouble with the Kirk for having a shoulder of mutton roasted on a Sunday morning; another for powdering his wig on that most holy of days."

Going to School

Most parishes in Scotland had a small village school. Often it was just one schoolroom heated by an open peat fire. The schooling was usually very basic. With classes as large as 70, it was difficult for the teacher to do little more than teach simple reading, writing and arithmetic.

Children from wealthy families went to grammar schools and academies where the fees were high. The main subjects in grammar schools were Latin, Greek and History. Academies offered more practical subjects such as science, maths and modern languages. Even children who worked in the mills were sent to school for two hours every day. In the **slum** districts of the growing cities, there were free 'ragged' schools to teach the children of the poorest families. They were taught reading and writing and also useful skills that would help them get a job such as woodcarving and cookery.

"At seven the pupils had religious instruction, followed by geography and natural history until nine. Thereafter they were given a breakfast of porridge and milk. The morning was spent on industrial training – making nets and teasing hair for mattresses. In the afternoon – reading, writing and arithmetic."

A day in a ragged school in 1845

Exploring further – Daily life

During the nineteenth century, education changed across Britain. Discover more about changes outside Scotland. Follow this path on the CD-ROM:

Exploring the Wider World > Focus On: Victorian Britain > Education.

The Highland Clearances

The Jacobites were totally defeated at Culloden in 1746. Many were executed, imprisoned or **exiled** to the Americas. The Highland countryside was patrolled by government troops in case of future trouble. Highlanders were forbidden to own weapons, play the bagpipes or wear tartan. Chiefs lost many of their powers – the old clan way of life came to an end.

There were no more risings in support of the Stuarts. Clan chiefs began to think more about trade and making money from their lands, instead of fighting and rebellion. Chiefs no longer needed loyal fighting men and they stopped counting their wealth in warriors. After 1760 they wanted skilled farmers who would pay them high rents in cash.

Before 1745, most people in Scotland lived as farmers in the countryside. After 1760 however, more Scots lived in towns and had to buy their food. Highland chiefs knew they could profit from farming their land in modern ways. Much of the Highlands was well suited for herding large flocks of a new breed of sheep, the Cheviot. However the families who used to farm in the clachans or villages had to go. Their land was now needed by the new sheep farmers. In glen after glen, the old **rig** farms were swept away and the people were 'cleared' from the land.

The Cheviot was a hardy animal that produced more meat and finer wool than the smaller native sheep. It could forage well in the Highland glens.

Dozens of ruined cottages from the time of the Clearances can still be seen in most Highland glens today.

The worst 'clearances' were in Strathnaver on land owned by the Countess of Sutherland. She used managers or factors to evict the local people and run her new 'improved' estate. In 1814 her factor Patrick Sellar used great cruelty in clearing the people from the land. Homes and grazing land were burned to force the people out. Sellar was eventually tried for the murder of an old woman who could not leave her burning home.

In other areas, police and soldiers were used to throw the people out of their homes. The women of Strathcarron were beaten and kicked by the police in 1854 when they refused to leave. Most Highlanders quietly accepted their fate. They could not fight against their clan chiefs. They had no weapons and no other leaders. Their church ministers even told them to obey the law and said that the loss of their family homes and land was simply 'God's Will'.

An eyewitness account of clearances in Sutherland in 1819

"The constables rushed on the houses of the people and immediately began to set fire to them till about three hundred homes were in flames. Little or no time was given for the removal of persons or property. The people tried to remove the sick and the helpless before the fire reached them."

Exploring further – An agricultural revolution

The Highland Clearances were not the only change that took place in Scottish farming. Explore other changes on the CD-ROM. Follow this path:

Exploring Scotland > Discoveries, Inventions and Ideas > Changes on the land.

New lives in new lands

Thousands of Highland families were cleared from their farmland in the years between 1760 and 1885. Some were rehoused by the landowners in planned coastal villages such as Plockton and Ullapool. They tried to make a new living from herring fishing. Others moved to crofts, or small farms, on the coast. Many moved to the crowded factory towns in central Scotland.

Most of the Highland folk struggled in their new homes. Many of the fishing families starved when the herring shoals moved away from Scotland's coasts. The crofters found they had been given land with poor soil but still had to pay high rents to the landowners. Lowland Scots in towns such as Glasgow often treated the Gaelic speaking incomers from the Highlands as aliens. This made it hard for them to find well-paid work.

More than a hundred thousand Highlanders left Scotland for a new life in America, Canada, or even further afield in Australia or New Zealand.

Emigrants faced a long, desperate journey by sailing ship. The Highlanders were crammed beneath the decks for up to twelve weeks. When their own supplies ran out, the ship masters charged them high prices for fresh water and food. Many emigrants were drowned in sea-storms. Others fell ill from scurvy and dysentery.

Those who survived the sea journey found that life was very hard in their new homeland. Good farmland was scarce so wild forest had to be cleared. Good tools and crop seed were expensive. Many Highland families starved in their first winter in North America. Only help from other Gaelic folk who had settled earlier kept many of these **emigrants** alive.

From an advert for ships to America, 1839

"Opportunities for Farmers and Mechanics who wish to secure their passage to North America in a first-class ship. Emigrants may be sure that every attention will be paid to their comfort and safety. Also land for purchase in Ohio at the rate of One British Pound per acre. Apply to Mr Thomas Cochran, Advocate in Aberdeen."

In time, the hard working Highland Scots built new successful lives for themselves overseas. Placenames in Canada such as New Glasgow and Campbellton show where the Scots settlers put down new roots. Many Scots became important people in their new countries. John MacDonald left the Highlands as a boy but became the first Prime Minister of Canada.

Many Highland men found another way of making a living once the old clan ways of life disappeared. They joined new Scottish regiments in the British Army such as the Black Watch and the Gordon Highlanders. Highland soldiers fought against the French in America, India and Africa, helping Britain to win an enormous Empire of rich **colonies** overseas. At the start of Queen Victoria's reign in 1837, more than a quarter of the men in the British Army were Highlanders.

The Black Watch regiment was founded in 1739. This Highland unit got its name from its dark tartan that was very different from the English redcoats.

Exploring further – Life in America

Many Scots emigrated to America. Life there was very different. Parts of the continent were only just being explored. Follow this path on the CD-ROM to find out more: Exploring the Wider World > Focus On: The Wild West.

Life in the slums

After 1840, workers flooded into Scotland's cities from the Lowland countryside, the Highlands and famine-stricken Ireland. These newcomers hoped to find good jobs with high wages. However many desperate people were seeking work at the same time, so employers could pay very low wages. Most of the new workers had to live in the cheapest places they could find. These were the rotting houses in the **slum** districts.

Most working families were crowded into one-roomed flats in **tenements**. The rooms were often too small for a bed so families had to sleep on straw on the ground. Many of the flats had no windows and bad air collected in them. Rats and other vermin infested most of these crumbling buildings. There were no toilets and no running water, so it was difficult to keep clean. In winter, the rooms were damp and difficult to heat.

There were no sewers or drains in the slum districts. People took their water from a **standpipe** in the street. They left their own waste in **midden** piles in the open courts between the slums. Dwelling houses were often next door to tanneries and slaughterhouses that produced evil smells and poisonous material. Animal dung, blood and intestines were just poured into the street drains. When it rained, all kinds of rubbish was swept down from the streets into the basement flats where the poorest workers lived. In these conditions, disease was common.

 Conditions were extremely cramped in the tenement slums and with no fresh water, it was very difficult to keep clean and healthy.

Disease

Overcrowding and the lack of fresh air meant that tuberculosis thrived in the slums. This was a deadly infection that attacked the lungs. Thousands of Victorian Scots died from this wasting illness. Others caught killer diseases such as typhoid and cholera. They broke out when human waste got into the drinking water used by the slum dwellers. Cholera killed thousands of Scots in three big **epidemics** in 1832, 1848 and 1853. So many died in Glasgow that new cemeteries were opened and pits dug to hold the dead.

Things only improved after 1850 when Town Councils began to clear away the worst of the slums and the middens, and to build underground pipes and sewers. Glasgow Town Council also built magnificent **aqueducts** to carry fresh water from Loch Katrine to the city.

Magazines like *Punch* tried to alert their middle-class readers to the horrors of disease in working-class districts.

A COURT FOR KING CHOLERA.

A doctor's report on Greenock in 1840

"In one part of Market Street is a dunghill. It is never removed. There is a tenement next to it and in the summer each house swarms with flies. Food and drink must be covered. If left exposed for a minute, the flies attack it and it is rendered unfit for use from the strong taste of the dunghill left by the flies."

Exploring further – Key people

Discover more about those who helped to improve people's lives during the Industrial Revolution. Follow this path on the CD-ROM:

Biographies > Lord Shaftesbury or Doctor Barnardo.

Doon the Clyde

The world's first paddle steamer sailed across Dalswinton Loch near Dumfries in 1788 at a speed of five miles per hour. In 1802 its inventor, William Symington, had built the *Charlotte Dundas*, a powerful steamboat for pulling coal barges along the Forth & Clyde canal between Edinburgh and Glasgow. However Symington's revolutionary boat was not popular with the canal owners. They feared that the wash from its paddles would damage their canal banks.

The world's first successful passenger steamship was *The Comet* that ran from Port Glasgow to the Broomielaw in central Glasgow in 1812. By 1840 a fleet of steam paddle ships worked their trade along the Firth of Clyde. It became common for Glaswegians to take a day trip 'doon the watter' to holiday resorts such as Dunoon and Rothesay. Larger steamships called puffers carried important supplies such as coal to the Hebrides or to northern Scotland via the Caledonian Canal.

Shipbuilding

Victorian Clydeside soon became world famous for building ships. The engineer Robert Napier from Dumbarton founded the Cunard company which built passenger ocean liners. Cunard's first liner, *Britannia*, crossed the Atlantic in a record time of ten days in 1840. Napier's engines were so well built and reliable that the Royal Navy used them in their new steam battleships, the 'Ironclads'.

 Victorian shipbuilders like John Scott Russell took great pride in the skill and craftsmanship of the Scottish shipyards.

By 1860 there were many ship building companies on the Clyde. They employed thousands of skilled men who had mastered the special crafts needed in shipbuilding. Clydeside companies developed new technologies such as building hulls from light steel plates. The world's first sea-worthy steel vessel, *SS Rotomahana*, was launched on the Clyde in 1879.

Not all of the ships built in Victorian Scotland were steel steamships. The fastest, and the loveliest, were the wooden clipper sailing ships that ran from Britain to the far eastern **colonies** and to Australia.

Each year Scottish newspaper readers enjoyed following the clipper races as these sleek ships raced to be the first to bring their cargo to the London market. The record holder on the Shanghai route was the Aberdeen-built  *SS Thermopylae*, which beat Dumbarton's *Cutty Sark* by four days in 1870. There was no doubt in the minds of the proud Victorian public that the best ships in the world were built in Scotland.

In full sail clippers, like the *Cutty Sark*, could cover more than four hundred miles per day, carrying light but valuable cargoes such as Chinese tea.

From *A History of Scottish Shipbuilding* by W Donaldson

"Shipbuilding built whole new towns in Scotland. There were only fields at Clydebank until J & G Thomson's moved their yard there from Govan in 1871. By 1902, over 18,000 people lived there."

Exploring further – Searching the age of revolutions

To find out more about the eighteenth and nineteenth centuries click on Search on the top panel of the Contents page. Pick a word from the keywords on the next page and click on Enter. A list of pages on the CD-ROM that mention this word will appear. Click on the names of the pages to find out what they show.

An age of improvement

The years between 1700 and 1900 saw many changes in Scotland, starting with the union with England and the Jacobite rebellions. New towns and industries sprung up. This upheaval had many terrible results for poorer Scots such as low wages, **slum** housing, poverty and disease.

After 1860 more Scottish workers belonged to Trade Unions. The Unions fought to get better and safer conditions for their members. By 1880 many Scottish workers were better paid and had shorter working hours than before. The burghs slowly became much cleaner. New houses had to have running water and flush toilets.

There were great advances in medicine in Victorian Scotland. Sir James Simpson in Edinburgh was the first doctor to use chloroform to put patients to sleep during operations. By 1900 Scotland's hospitals were amongst the most modern in the world.

Scotland and Empire

By 1880 Britain had an Empire that stretched across every part of the globe. The Scots were very proud of the part their small country had played in making Britain so powerful. After London, Glasgow was the 'Second City of the Empire'. Its skilled people and industries had helped turn Britain into the 'Workshop of the World'.

Alexander Graham Bell

Victorian Scots were pioneers in science and technology. Alexander Graham Bell made the first working telephone in 1875. His Bell Telephone Company became one of the biggest businesses in the United States in the 1880s.

Many Scots went to the **colonies** as missionaries, hoping to do good works and spread the Christian faith. David Livingstone from Blantyre began life as a mill worker but studied medicine and became a missionary in Africa in 1840. Another surprising millworker was Mary Slessor who was born in Aberdeen but worked in the **jute** factories of Dundee as a young girl. She worked for many years among the people of Calabar in West Africa who knew her as 'The Great Mother'.

In 1888 the Glasgow Exhibition took place. Almost six million people, including Queen Victoria, visited its pavilions. They celebrated Scotland's achievements in science and engineering. There were many new inventions on display including the electricity that lit the Exhibition. The Scots who visited were proud to be Victorians.

"No-one who visits the Exhibition will fail to be impressed and amazed by the ways in which this great city lies at the heart of the Empire. Natives of a hundred colonies from the Arctic Canada to the deepest jungles of Africa and Asia have the words 'Made in Glasgow' imprinted upon their daily lives."

From a Glasgow newspaper in 1888

Exploring further – The Great Exhibition

The Glasgow Exhibition of 1888 followed the Great Exhibition in London in 1851. Follow this path to find out more about this celebration of Britain and the British Empire: Exploring the Wider World > Focus On: Victorian Britain > Prince Albert and the Great Exhibition.

Timeline

1707	Union of Scotland and England to form United Kingdom of Great Britain
1715	George of Hanover becomes King of Britain
	Jacobite rising led by the Earl of Mar fails
1720s	London Government builds forts and roads to quiet the Highlands
1730s	Farming methods change – fields become bigger, fertilizer used
1745	Jacobite rising led by Bonnie Prince Charlie
1746	16 April – Highland clans defeated and slaughtered at Culloden Moor
1759	Cardell, Garbett and Roebuck set up Carron Iron Works near Falkirk
1760s	New Town Edinburgh starts to develop
1765	James Watt designs the first successful steam engine
1770s	Cloth-making factories and mills take over from home industry
1775	Forth to Clyde canal from Grangemouth to Glasgow opened
1792	William Murdoch perfects his gas-light system
1812	Kilmarnock to Troon railway opened
1814	Highland Clearances force many Scots off their land – Strathnaver clearances in Sutherland
1847	Caledonian canal completed
1862	Strathcarron clearances in Wester Ross
1875	Alexander Graham Bell makes his first working telephone
1888	Glasgow Exhibition
1890	Firth of Forth Rail-Bridge opened

Glossary

aqueducts   bridges designed to carry water across the landscape

artillery   large cannon and other guns used by the army

blasphemer   someone who swears using God or Christ's name

Catholic   Christian who belongs to the Roman Catholic Church

Central Belt   middle part of Scotland in the Forth and Clyde valleys between Edinburgh and Glasgow

clansmen   members of a Highland clan such as the MacGregors

colonies   lands overseas that were part of the British Empire such as Canada and Australia

emigrants   people who left Scotland to settle overseas and build a new life abroad

epidemic   widespread outbreak of a dangerous disease

exiled   ordered to leave your own country and not able to return

fermtoun   Scots name for villages where land was farmed in strips

flax   tough grass crop that can be turned into linen cloth

galleon   wooden sailing ship of the 17th and 18th centuries

jute   plant grown in India but sent to the mills in Dundee to be turned into rope and sacks

Kirk   Scots word for a church and for the Church of Scotland

mauled   to be badly beaten

midden   ancient word for heaps of rubbish, food and toilet waste

monarch   another name for a king or queen

navvies   nickname for the navigators, the men who planned and dug out the canal and railway routes in the 19th century

neo-classical   popular style in 18th century fashion, art and architecture that copied the Romans and Greeks

ore   rock that contains flecks of metal and other precious minerals

Protestant   Christian who belongs to one of the reformed churches of northern Europe such as the Church of Scotland

raw materials   raw goods such as cotton fibre which are imported into Britain to be turned into manufactured goods

repentance   act of feeling genuinely sorry for one's misbehaviour

revolution   sudden change which affects peoples lives dramatically

rigs   small strips of land shared out amongst the farming people in the old Scottish fermtouns before 1750

Sabbath   biblical name for Sunday

slum   poor quality housing that was often built using cheap materials

standard   another name for a flag, usually a royal or princely one

standpipe   water pipe and tap in the street

tenement   traditional Scots town buildings with up to 10 or 11 stories

Union of the Crowns   event in 1603 when James VI of Scotland also became King of England as James I

wynds   narrow unlit lanes between the tenements in Edinburgh's Old Town

Index

Titles in the *Explore Scottish History* series include:

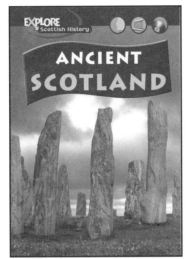

Hardback   0 431 14520 2

Hardback   0 431 14522 9

Hardback   0 431 14524 5

Hardback   0 431 14526 1

Hardback   0 431 14530 x

Find out about the other titles in this series on our website www.heinemann.co.uk/library